The Water Cycle

by Helen Frost

Consulting Editor: Gail Saunders-Smith, Ph.D.

Reviewer: Carolyn M. Tucker
Water Education Specialist
California Department of Water Resources

Pebble Books

an imprint of Capstone Press
Mankato, Minnesota

Pebble Books are published by Capstone Press
151 Good Counsel Drive, P.O. Box 669, Mankato, Minnesota 56002
http://www.capstone-press.com

2 3 4 5 6 04 03 02 01 00

Library of Congress Cataloging-in-Publication Data
Frost, Helen, 1949–
    The water cycle/by Helen Frost.
    p. cm.—(Water)
    Includes bibliographical references and index.
    Summary: Simple text and photographs describe the stages of the water cycle.
    ISBN 0-7368-0409-9
    1. Hydrologic cycle—Juvenile literature. [1. Hydrologic cycle.] I. Title.
II. Series: Frost, Helen, 1949– Water.
GB848.F76   2000
551.48—dc21   99-12968
                                                                    CIP

Note to Parents and Teachers

The Water series supports national science standards for
understanding the properties of water. This book describes and
illustrates the water cycle. The photographs support early readers in
understanding the text. This book introduces early readers to
subject-specific vocabulary words, which are defined in the Words
to Know section. Early readers may need assistance to read some
words and to use the Table of Contents, Words to Know, Read
More, Internet Sites, and Index/Word List sections of the book.

Table of Contents

Water 5

Evaporation 9

Condensation 13

Precipitation 17

The Water Cycle 21

Words to Know 22

Read More 23

Internet Sites 23

Index/Word List. 24

Water moves and changes in the water cycle. A cycle has no beginning and no end.

Some water is in oceans, lakes, and rivers. Some water is underground.

The sun heats water.
Heat changes water from
a liquid into a vapor.
This action is evaporation.

Water vapor rises into the air. Water vapor is a gas you cannot see.

Water vapor cools as it rises. The water vapor turns back into a liquid. This action is condensation.

Condensation can form clouds. Clouds are dust and tiny drops of water.

Water from clouds can fall to the ground as precipitation. Rain and snow are two kinds of precipitation.

Some precipitation soaks into the ground. Some precipitation falls into oceans, lakes, and rivers.

Water moves from the ground to the air. The water falls back to the ground in a different place. The water cycle goes on forever.

Words to Know

condensation—the action of turning from a gas into a liquid; water vapor turns into liquid water when it condenses.

cycle—something that happens over and over again; water changes its form over and over again in the water cycle; the same amount of water is always moving and changing in the water cycle.

evaporation—the action of a liquid changing into a gas; heat causes water to evaporate.

precipitation—water that falls from clouds; precipitation can be rain, hail, sleet, or snow.

soak—to wet thoroughly; some precipitation soaks into the ground.

water vapor—water in the form of a gas; water vapor is tiny drops of water that cannot be seen.

Read More

Berger, Melvin and Gilda Berger. *Water, Water Everywhere: A Book about the Water Cycle.* Discovery Readers. Philadelphia: Chelsea House Publishers, 1999.

Jacobs, Marian B. *Why Does It Rain?* Library of Why? New York: PowerKids Press, 1999.

Saunders-Smith, Gail. *Rain.* Weather. Mankato, Minn.: Pebble Books, 1998.

Internet Sites

Earth's Water
http://wwwga.usgs.gov/edu/mearth.html

Simple Water Science
http://www.epa.gov/OGWDW/kids/tuar.html

The Water Cycle at Work
http://www.epa.gov/ogwdw/kids/cycle.html

Index/Word List

air, 11, 21
clouds, 15, 17
condensation,
   13, 15
cools, 13
cycle, 5, 21
dust, 15
evaporation, 9
fall, 17,
   19, 21

flows, 19
gas, 11
ground, 17,
   19, 21
heats, 9
lakes, 7, 19
liquid, 9, 13
oceans, 7, 19
precipitation,
   17, 19

rain, 17
rises, 11, 13
rivers, 7, 19
snow, 17
soaks, 19
sun, 9
underground,
   7
vapor, 9,
   11, 13

Word Count: 146
Early-Intervention Level: 13

Editorial Credits
Mari C. Schuh, editor; Timothy Halldin, cover designer; Linda Clavel, illustrator;
   Kimberly Danger, photo researcher

Photo Credits
ColePhoto/Mark E. Gibson, 10
David and Tess Young/TOM STACK & ASSOCIATES, 8
David F. Clobes, 1
Index Stock Imagery, cover
International Stock/Victor Ramos, 6
Photri-Microstock, 20; Photri-Microstock/Kenneth Martin, 12; Fotopic, 16
Robert McCaw, 14
Unicorn Stock Photos/H. H. Thomas, 18